colour, texture, form and tone, as well as skills in using tools, materials and media.

Design and Technology not only provides a meaningful framework in which young children can develop these concepts, skills and attitudes, but also enables them to experiment with, control, and change the relationships they have with their environment in ways which enhance their efficiency and self-image.

Design and Technological activity is directed towards developing children who are able to understand their environment - the natural, the made, and the social - and looking at how they interact within it. This means looking at:

- How the environment affects them and how they affect it.
- How they can control certain factors within their environment but not others.
- How they can change their environment for the better, and how they can improve it for others as well as themselves.

Design and Technology is mutually supportive with all other areas of the curriculum. It would be difficult to isolate any of the elements in the Programme of Study as uniquely supporting Design and Technology. It is a curriculum area which draws on the concepts and skills related to other curriculum areas, but also provides a rich source of activities to further develop these same skills and concepts.

Scientific concepts such as force, gravity, and control; mathematical skills such as estimation, and collecting data; mathematical concepts such as shape and space; linguistic skills in developing and using an accurate and appropriate vocabulary related to materials, tools and processes: these are all inherent in the activities which the young child will encounter through carrying out Design and Technology.

The content of the Design and Technology curriculum also enables the teacher to select activities with which the young child is already familiar, and to build on these experiences in a way that provides continuity and progression. Pre-school experience for many children will enable them to have access to stories, to role-play, to making simple choices, and to expressing their own ideas through a variety of media such as drawing, painting, talking, and using construction equipment.

These experiences will provide a foundation for the child and the teacher to build on, enabling the child to change from being a passive participant in these activities towards becoming an initiator and an active participant in making decisions about their immediate environment. The young children will make this transition with confidence and competence if their development is supported by activities which they enjoy, which are constantly stimulating them, and which enable them to develop the necessary skills and concepts. Design and Technology can provide this developmental framework and in a context which the child will find both stimulating and enjoyable.

DEVELOPING VISUAL AND PERCEPTUAL SKILLS

The ability to look and see, that is the development of observational skills, is an essential foundation for the creative process. As children look more closely and critically at objects they can begin to analyse in terms of line, shape, colour, texture, form, structure, size and function. Identifying these attributes, and their interrelationship, is fundamental to understanding both the natural and the made environment.

The Programme of Study for Key Stage 1 in Design and Technology includes elements at all levels which draw on observational skills.

In order to build up their analytical visual skills children need regular opportunities for observational

Design and Technology	Programme of Study *Satisfying Needs and Addressing Opportunities*

'Evaluate familiar things by observing and describing them, saying what they [children] like or dislike about them and why people have or need them.'

Design and Technology	*Developing and Using Artefacts, Systems and Environments*

'Recognise pattern in the structure of objects.'

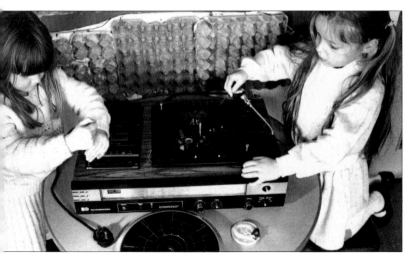

work throughout the early years, starting as soon as the child enters school. Their observations can be directly translated through a variety of materials and media, although recorded observations may not always be the most effective way to support children in identifying and discriminating between the different attributes that they find. Activities in sorting and classifying may provide a more accessible means of demonstrating their understanding of what they can see and identify in terms of attributes.

Whether the activity involves recording, or simply takes the form of a discussion, the role of the teacher is crucial to the quality of the experience that the child has. The way that the child is introduced to the artefact or item to be observed is important. Through careful questioning the teacher will be able to draw the child's attention to a number of important factors related to the size, shape, texture, and inherent structure of an object.

- What are we looking at?
- What is the purpose of each part of it?
- What might it be made of?
- What are the inherent shapes?
- How do they relate to each other?
- Is it natural or has it been made?
- How might it differ from others of its kind?

It is important for the child to study each part of an item or area closely, as well as seeing it as a whole. It may also be useful for the child to experience the tactile qualities of an object, as sensory experience will enhance the quality of information that the child gains about form, shape, scale, temperature and weight.

Sorting as an observational activity

Sorting activities provide opportunities to develop in children key skills - identification, discrimination, and classification - which enable them to identify inherent properties of objects, and to separate or group them according to those attributes using similarity or difference as a basis. These skills are vital in enabling children to order and to understand relationships in both the natural and the made environment.

Structured sorting apparatus, such as Diennes Logiblocs, will provide initial experiences in recognizing basic attributes of colour, shape and size. This will, however, offer only limited experiences in developing concepts related to the environment.

It is important that children use unstructured collections such as shells, nuts, buttons, leaves, pebbles, and stamps. A resource of unstructured materials can be collected by the children from their own environment, and will offer a rich source for them to investigate and identify attributes such as texture, pattern, form, weight, smell, and taste. It will also provide a tangible link with their own, made and natural environment.

Children should be encouraged to identify attributes themselves, making their own attribute cards/indicators. A supply of string will enable them to define attribute areas, and allows for flexibility in creating mixed sub-sets since the attribute areas are easily manipulated.

INTRODUCTION

The advent of Design and Technology in the National Curriculum was both positive and supportive to early years education. It not only recognized the value of many of the activities already being carried out in classrooms, such as role-play, investigative and observational activities, and creative work with a wide variety of materials, it also helped teachers to integrate these activities into the curriculum in a more planned and meaningful way.

The developmental needs of the young child are complex and varied. The importance of play and of first-hand experiences have been widely acknowledged. Children are constantly interacting with the world that they encounter every day, and their environment both in and out of school, and trying to make sense of it.

The concepts, skills, and attitudes developed at this stage are crucial to the quality of later development, and it is through structured play and first-hand practical activity that this early development is best supported.

Through play children are experimenting and developing ideas, isolating problems and dealing with them. They are developing initiatives and positive attitudes in their relationships with their peers. They are beginning to use language to develop and evaluate ideas, as well as responding critically to the ideas of others.

Through practical first-hand experience children are developing critical awareness of line, shape, pattern,

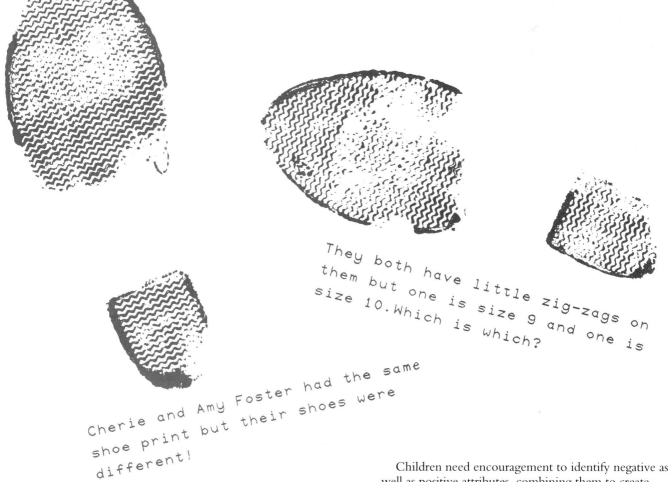

They both have little zig-zags on them but one is size 9 and one is size 10. Which is which?

Cherie and Amy Foster had the same shoe print but their shoes were different!

John says that there are boxes circles and stripes on his shoe print

Children need encouragement to identify negative as well as positive attributes, combining them to create sub-sets. Only when combining attributes in discrimination and classification are children beginning to develop concepts of form, structure, and function, as well as a growing appreciation of the complexity and sophistication of their environment.

Sorting shoes
Ask each child to take off one shoe and place these in a pile. These shoes can then be sorted using a variety of criteria such as:

- left/right
- laced/velcro/buckle/other fastening
- weight (choose one shoe [x], all others are either heavier or lighter than [x])
- colour
- size
- sole pattern
- shiny/dull

Investigating the different kinds of patterns on the sole can be carried out by taking a print off it first, and then asking each child to describe it.

The children may also be able to identify criteria of their own. For example, some shoes have small holes punched in them to form a pattern; some shoes have applied decoration such as bows; some shoes have words printed on them; some laced shoes have different numbers of holes for the laces.

Drawing as an observational activity
The act of recording observations through drawing is a means for children to reiterate what they have discussed with the teacher about an object. All the observations made through discussion can be recalled by the child and

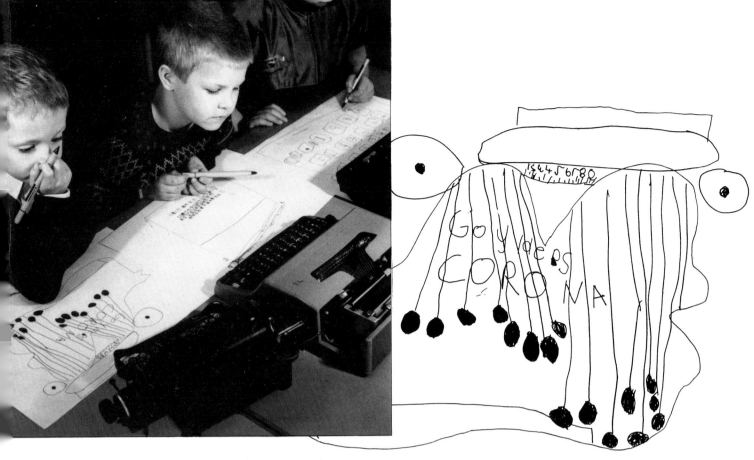

made concrete by recording them with pen or pencil onto paper.

Discussion will still be an important part of this stage of the activity, and it will be supportive for the children if their attention is directed towards certain features of the object again.

Observing and drawing typewriters

For this activity the children were presented with four different typewriters: a toy plastic typewriter, an antique typewriter, a modern manual typewriter, and a modern electronic typewriter. Initial discussion concentrated on the relative differences between them:

- what kind of materials had been used to make each typewriter?
- did they all have a similar weight?
- could they be ranked in order of size?
- were the keyboard layouts the same?
- what was the function of each part, and how did they relate to each other visually?
- what was the meaning of any other graphics on each typewriter?
- did the carriage move across on all of them, and if not why not?

After a general discussion about all the machines, attention was then drawn to the structural detail of each one individually:

- how were the keys joined to the machine?
- what happened when a key was depressed?
- did the paper feed in at the same place on each typewriter?
- did the typewriter have a handle to carry it?
- what shapes were the different parts of the machine?
- how did the shape change if you walked around the table?

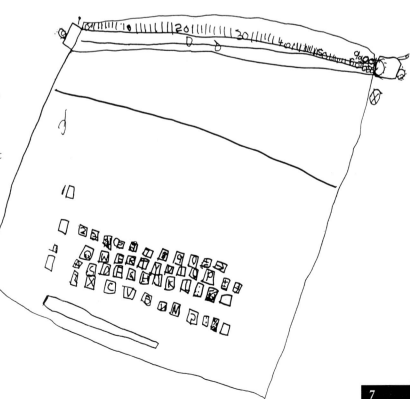

The recordings that the children made may not necessarily reflect the quality of the observation, and this can only be assessed through the quality of the discussion that the teacher has with each child. A drawing may reflect how carefully the child has observed the

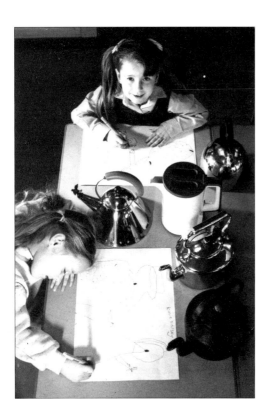

direction, and changes of direction, in line. It may also reflect the use of shape in an object, but not the form since this relies on the ability to use perspective. It may reflect proportion, and the interrelationship of component parts. It may also show several planes in the same drawing, and this may be a reflection of the child either moving around the object, or moving the object around, and not necessarily because their perception is immature.

After the child has completed the drawing it is helpful to talk through the content with them while comparing the information in the recording with the information they can gain from direct observation.

Painting as an observational activity

Using painting to record observations enables a child to interpret and record what they see in terms of colour and tone. If the child is going to develop this skill they will need to have experience with paint which provides continuity and progression in observing, mixing, and applying colours.

Observing and painting a bowl of fruit

Before children can observe and interpret colour accurately they need to have an understanding of it in terms of being able to identify main colours correctly, and to understand how secondary colours are formed from primary colours.

Using a paint palette which uses only the primary range will support children in developing their skills in mixing any secondary colours that they need. It is important that children are given adequate time to mix and remix until they are satisfied with the colour they have made. They also need a clean palette that enables them to keep their first colours pure.

For this activity the children first discussed the contents of a large bowl of mixed fruit. The items of fruit were chosen so that two of them were primary colours (red apple and yellow lemon), and two were secondary colours (green apples and oranges). Colour charts from paint manufacturers can be a useful aid in this activity, enabling the children to identify a tonal equivalent, and then to try to match it with their paint.

Attention to shape, spatial relationships, and proportion is important too, and the teacher's support throughout the activity will ensure that these attributes are considered.

Recording with three-dimensional media

Observations can be made using a variety of three-dimensional media. This is particularly supportive for children experiencing difficulty developing concepts related to spatial relationships. Using clay to record the bowl of fruit enabled proportion, form, position and shape to be interpreted in a concrete form. While this is a valuable method of recording observations, it can also provide a useful and supportive prerequisite to the painting or drawing activity, as it will enable the child to have observed the object, and to have 'seen' it with their hands as well as their eyes.

DEVELOPING SPATIAL AWARENESS

The development of spatial awareness in children fulfils several objectives.

- It enables children to understand how they relate to a space that they are in, for example, their playground, their classroom, or their bedroom, and to other objects in that area.
- It enables children to understand how objects in that space relate to each other in terms of size, shape, position and scale.
- It enables children to plan potential change in that area using mental manipulation or modelling with a scale medium.
- It enables children to understand what space is made up of or defined by.

The development of these skills and concepts using a scale medium, such as construction equipment, will support the children in using the same skills in life-size contexts.

It would be unusual to find an infant or a nursery teaching area without any construction equipment. It is one of the most useful, and possibly underused, resources available to the young child. Play and structured activities with construction equipment can develop a variety of manipulative and intellectual skills, as well as concepts which deal with the spatial relationships of shapes, spaces, and form.

Building with construction equipment can enable a child to understand how the component parts of a structure begin to relate to each other in space. Ideas and plans can be investigated, tested, and adapted easily in a concrete way. Children are able to control the outcome of their actions, defining and redefining until satisfied with the final result.

The extensive range of commercial construction equipment and kits gives a wide choice, and can offer children a broad experience of different forms and methods of joining components. There are, however, several important factors to be considered concerning the use of construction equipment as a meaningful resource. This wide range will enable teachers to consider a variety of criteria before planning activities for their children.

- How do the pieces join together, if at all? Children need to develop their manipulative skills with equipment which allows ease of joining and separating component parts. Force should not be necessary.
- Do the parts stay securely fixed during the activity? How durable is the structure?
- Does the activity enable the child to build on previous experience in the development of skills and concepts?
- Does the range of activities enable the child to work in a variety of social contexts, for example in a small group or individually?

- Do the activities enable the children to develop their own ideas as well as following a directed path?
- Are the kits gender-free?

The children will need to have access to a specific vocabulary related to construction work. They will develop this vocabulary most effectively through conversation with the teacher, and then with their peers. This vocabulary might include terms such as:

parts	nut	tall(er)
join	bolt	short(er)
separate	plan	wide(r)
build	space	stable/firm
dismantle	frame	hinge
peg	teeth	base

Initial investigation and exploration of the attributes of any type of construction medium is important. The child will need time to play freely in order to fully understand how parts are joined and held together, as well as examining the variety of component parts. After this stage activities should be structured to ensure that the development of skills and concepts is sequential, and that each experience builds on the one before.

Technology games with construction equipment

Many teachers have a repertoire of games which they play with children to support mathematical and linguistic development. This repertoire will probably have been acquired over a period of time, and is continually added to and refined. The games often require a minimum of apparatus, and are usually carried out with the children seated in a circle.

'Know that a system is made of related parts which are combined for a purpose.'
'Recognize, and make models of, simple structures around them.'

There are many other games that can be played in this way, which will not only support those areas outlined above, but will also provide valuable experience to support the Design and Technology curriculum.

Games with construction equipment will enable children to explore the potential of the apparatus in a purposeful way as well as giving them the opportunity to express their observations and ideas verbally.

Building a group model (1)

A basket or box of construction equipment, such as Lego, PolyM, or Stickle bricks, is passed around the circle. The teacher starts by choosing one piece and saying 'This is our model, and it is a . . .'.

The next child selects and adds one piece, running through the statement again, but putting their own interpretation at the end. By carrying out this activity each child is looking at the interrelationship of the shapes, adding to them, and making their own interpretation of the structure.

Building a group model (2)

The nature of the model is defined by the teacher (or a child when more experienced with the game) and the statement then becomes 'This is our spaceship/monster/house/park and this part is the . . .'.

Each child is making a decision about their choice of component, what it represents, and where it will be situated on the model. It may be useful to start this game with a large base piece to enable other pieces to be attached firmly.

These games enable the children to work cooperatively as a class. The following activities are structured to enable them to develop ideas, concepts, and skills individually in the first one, and then work in small groups to try their ideas out on a larger scale.

A home for a pet

For this activity each child was given ten multilink cubes, and asked to create a 'pet' with them, and to name the pet. Their pet then needed a home, built out of construction equipment. This activity provided many opportunities for discussion with the child.

- Can you put a roof on, or are the walls too low?
- Can your pet see out or does it need a window?
- Can you make a home for your pet and a friend's pet? How much bigger does it need to be?
- Is there enough room for your pet to turn round?

Through this activity each child was developing concepts which deal with the interrelationship of size, shape, and space by constantly evaluating and re-evaluating their work against these criteria. The children were then asked to use construction equipment of a larger scale, and sheets of cardboard, and to use these ideas to construct a home for themselves. The same criteria were applied.

- Can you put a roof on, or are the walls too low?
- Can you see out or do you need a window?
- How many of you can fit inside comfortably?
- Are you able to move about or not?

It is important that each child is given an opportunity to articulate their response to each question as this will enable them to stimulate discussion within their own group, as well as helping them to clarify their own thoughts.

Analysis and reflection can be built in to any activity with construction equipment, and are fundamental if the child is to develop an understanding about the activity. A small display area in the classroom for 'models we have built today' can provide a fruitful source for this.

- Ask a child to draw his/her model or someone else's. Are they able to show how the different components are related to each other?
- Ask a child to copy another child's model so that it is identical.

Discuss the results of this with the child or the class.

The important feature of any activity with construction apparatus is that it is planned and structured to build on the child's previous experience, and that it enables further conceptual and physical development.

Developing spatial awareness through role play

A role-play area in the classroom can support the development of spatial awareness both through planning and setting it up, and through its use. In planning it children are creating an environment. They are generating proposals and designing a system. They are making decisions about the kind, number, size, and position of the components in that environment. By using it they are organizing equipment and resources in a defined area so that it is efficient. They are also organizing tasks related to that equipment and those resources. They will be sharing that area with others, and so they are constantly negotiating their role and their space within that environment.

It will be supportive to the children if the initial planning and setting up of this area follows a recognized procedure. This procedure could start with a whole-class discussion to decide what the area could be. The class is then divided into groups of four or five children and each group takes it in turn to plan an initial layout with any available resources. They draw up a list of other items needed, and may indicate where they might be placed in the area. Each proposal can be studied by the whole class, and the relative merits of each discussed.

By working within a recognized framework the children will be able to see that any decisions have been reached through a process of negotiation, taking the opinions and preferences of others into consideration.

The sandwich bar

In planning and setting up a sandwich bar for role-play activity a number of criteria were considered by the children related to their understanding and use of space.

- The sandwich bar needed a counter. Where could this be placed so that customers would know which side to stand at?
- If people wanted to eat their sandwiches inside where could they do this?
- What was the maximum number of customers that would be able to eat inside comfortably?
- If sandwich making followed a sequence, did the ingredients need to be displayed in that order?
- Would the customers be able to see the menu/price list/range of fillings from their side of the counter?
- If everyone wanted to be inside serving, or outside buying, how would this affect the organization of the activity?

Many of these criteria were only fully considered when the children started to use the area for role-play, and they began to encounter any inherent difficulty with decisions taken at an earlier stage of planning. As the children became more skilled at understanding and using space, they were also able to predict possible difficulties in their proposals, and make alternative suggestions without the need to experience it at first hand.

The children were, in effect, able to conceptualize the space and the components in it, and to manipulate them mentally in order to reach a satisfactory solution.

DEVELOPING SKILLS WITH MATERIALS

Children's experiences in recognizing and using different materials are varied when they start school. Whether they have had pre-school education or not, they are generally familiar with a limited range of materials, such as sand, water, clay and paper, and they may have little understanding of the characteristics of the materials they recognize.

With young children, it is necessary to extend their knowledge of characteristics, to enable them to use the range of materials that is available to them both efficiently and effectively. A useful starting point for this can be observing and discussing the children's immediate environment: the school building and the classroom. How many different materials can the children identify visually? Why is that particular material used for that purpose? Could another be substituted without any problems?

Children need experience in handling and discussing a variety of materials so that they can identify similarities and differences in properties.

Technology games with materials

While many teachers have developed a repertoire of games which they play with their children to support and enhance mathematical and linguistic development, this repertoire may not yet have been extended to include the Design and Technology curriculum.

Games which can be used to support the areas outlined above can also provide valuable experiences to support Design and Technology. Circle games are a useful and enjoyable activity which can extend vocabulary related to the properties of materials as well as extending understanding of those properties, and therefore inform choice in materials for Design and Technology activity.

Design and Technology	Programmes of Study *Working with Materials*
'Explore and use a variety of materials to design and make things.' 'Recognize that many materials are available and have different characteristics which make them appropriate for different tasks.' 'Investigate the properties of materials in the course of their designing and making.' 'Choose materials and equipment to make objects.'	

Circle games
Textile game
Samples of different textiles are distributed to groups of two or three children around the circle. Each group tries to think of two or three adjectives which apply to their sample. These adjectives are recorded on cards in front of each group for the whole circle to see.

Each group is then asked to select a word from another group which might apply to their sample. In this way the children will begin to identify similarities and differences between the different samples. The samples and the vocabulary can then be used to create a wall display which can be used as a point of reference for future work.

The range of samples might include textiles which are:

- rough
- smooth
- soft
- hard
- stretchy
- shiny
- sparkly
- knitted
- woven

as well as providing a comprehensive colour range.

The children may also create their own adjectives which will support discussion related to the visual and behavioural properties of this collection. Their own terms will provide a basis for discussion, and may also enable other adjectives to be introduced to them, such as transparent instead of see-through, rough or coarse instead of bumpy.

Mixed materials games

Similar games can be played using a variety of samples of resistant and non-resistant materials. It may be important to ensure that the use of a chosen material is not made too apparent by the form that the sample takes. The children can then be asked to specify uses of their own choosing without being unduly influenced by the object. For example, a piece of corriflute may provide a more fruitful sample of plastic than a comb which already embodies a purpose.

It may be useful if each group of children is asked to answer a set number of questions about their sample. For example:

- What does it feel like?
- What does it look like?
- What does it smell like?
- What do you think it is made of?
- What could you use it for?

These same questions can be put to the children privately, and their responses recorded either in writing or on audio cassette. A parent or classroom helper might be useful with this. The descriptions and samples can then be numbered correspondingly. The samples are distributed to the children, and one description read or played to the children, with each child or group trying to identify the correct sample. The children's own responses are more interesting and imaginative than those that might be compiled by an adult.

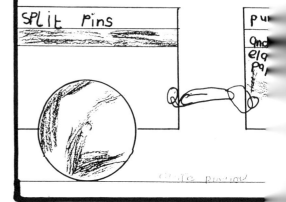

I fixed my wheels on with

SPLiT Pins

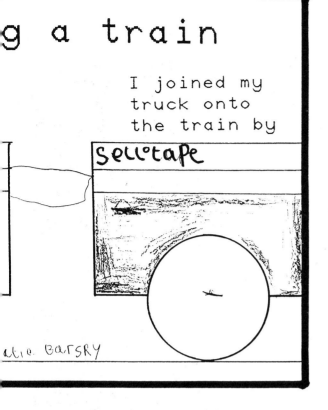

g a train

I joined my
truck onto
the train by

sellotape

atie Barsky

in

ined my
< onto
train by

q hole
ng qn
bnd qnd q
p

Joining materials together

As children develop their understanding of, and skills in handling different materials, they will look for ways to join those materials together when making things. So that they are aware of the wide range of ways that they might do this, it might be useful to devise activities which allow the children to concentrate on this.

Design and Technology	Programmes of Study *Developing and Using Artefacts, Systems and Environments*
'Recognize that materials can be linked in various ways to make or allow movement.'	

Before doing this the children will need to experience the materials and joining components in an investigative way. A supply of thin pieces of card and paper, a single hole punch, and a variety of joining components will allow the children to experiment, and devise simple fixings and joints. A range of components might include:

- rubber bands
- paper clips
- split pins
- treasury tags
- Sellotape
- string
- Pritt Stick
- tie-wires

These initial joining experiences can be focused on a sequence of linked units in thin card. For example, *a train*: each child has to join their truck on in a different way. Card wheels can also be attached to each truck using a different linking component.

A friendship line: each child has a figure made of thin card which they can personalize. They must then find a way of joining their figure onto the next one to create a linked row of figures.

If children are going to be encouraged to be efficient and autonomous in their designing activities, then it is important that they have a clear understanding of the range of resources and methods that are available to them in the classroom. Activities such as those already outlined will enable them to investigate those resources and methods in an enjoyable and meaningful way.

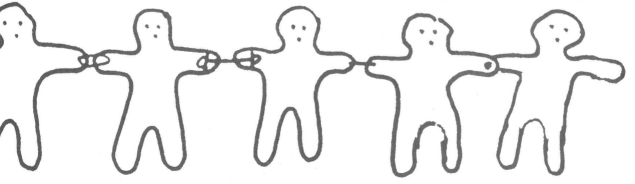

The washing line: the aim of this activity was to extend initial experiences that the children had had in investigating the characteristics of different materials, and ways of joining them together. As part of a role-play area in the classroom which was a launderette the children had created a wall display of a washing line. When the display was completed the children discussed how the washing was joined onto the line. Each child was asked to bring a peg in to school from home so that a comparison could be made between different kinds of pegs. This collection provided a starting point for comparing different ways of attaching washing to a line. Some pegs were wooden, some plastic, some involved a spring mechanism, and some were a push-on type. Some push-on pegs incorporated a serrated grip area, and some relied on a tight fit to keep the washing firmly attached.

The children were then asked to try and think of different ways that they could join washing onto a line. So that they would be able to develop and try out their ideas they each constructed a scaled-down washing line and mounted it on card. They would also make the 'washing' out of different materials and use available resources in the classroom to devise as many different ways of joining it onto their line as possible.

The first part of the children's practical work was to each construct a 'washing line'. Each child was given a piece of stiff card and asked to create a background garden for the washing line. The next step was to prepare the posts which would support the line. This involved the children in measuring section timber and cutting it to length both accurately and safely.

If children are relatively inexperienced with resistant materials then an activity like this, which involves a brief contact with the process of using a bench hook, vice, a saw, and glasspaper, may be an adequate experience on which to build and consolidate skills at a later stage.

The children then had to assess the length of string for their line, cut it, and tie it to the top of the posts. When this was complete, the children watched the teacher fix the lines to the background using a hot glue gun. The children then started to make the washing for their line, and to investigate ways of joining each piece to their line. Each child had been supplied with a small plastic spring peg as a starter, which gave them a feeling of initial success before developing some of their own ideas.

Some children made their lines longer than was necessary, so that when the lines were fixed, they hung down and sagged. One child then had the idea of making a clothes prop, as he said that his mother had one at home which she used to push up the line. The washing line slipped off the top when the prop was fixed, so the child drilled a hole in the end of the prop and made a groove for the line to fit into. The children chose to use paper, card, and vivelle (a paper-backed felt) to make their washing lines clothes, and used all the available linking components to join them onto their washing line.

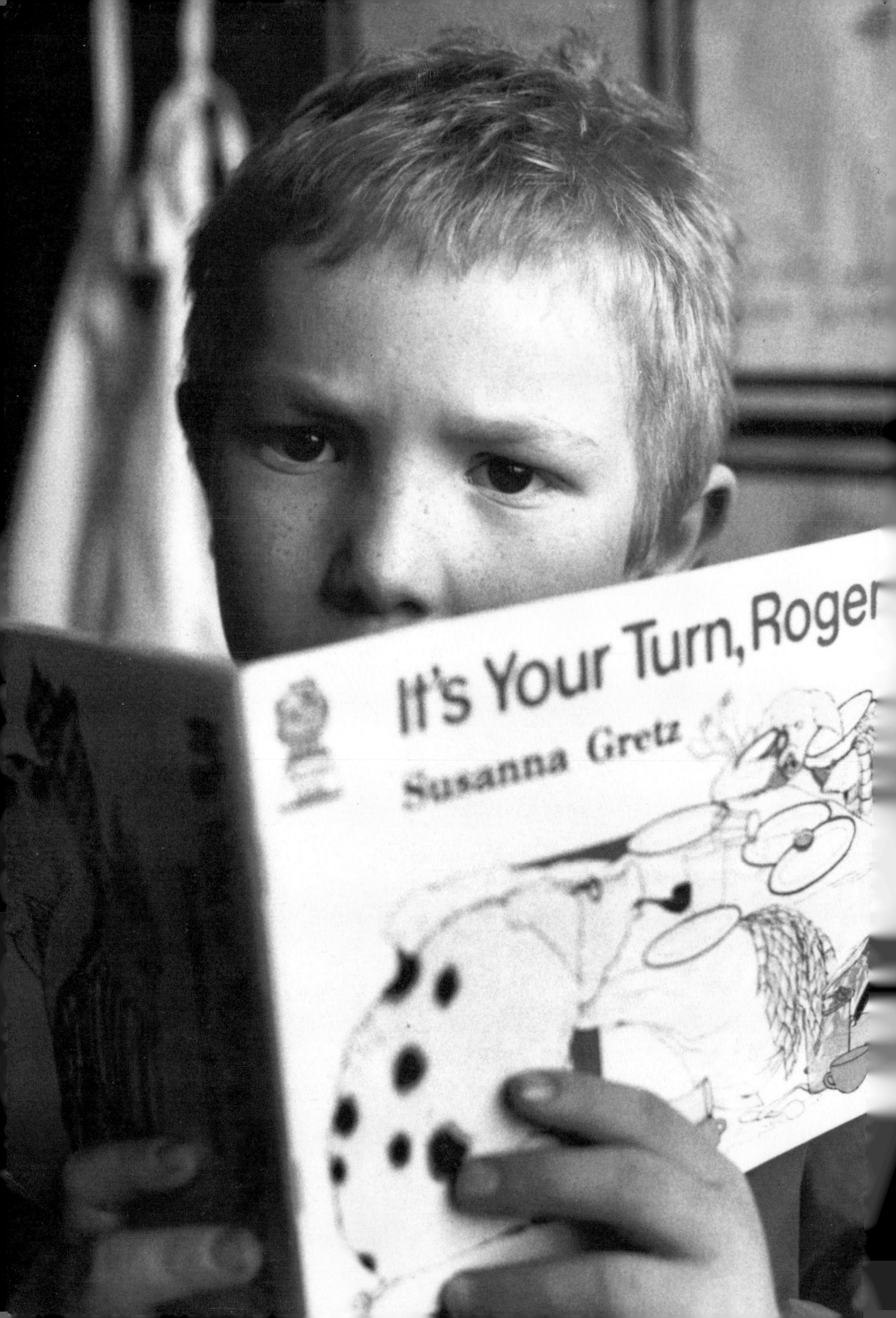
It's Your Turn, Roger
Susanna Gretz

STORY BOOKS AS CONTEXTS FOR DESIGN AND TECHNOLOGY

Story books provide an important focus for the young child, both as a listener, and as a teller. The characters and events in a picture book can lend meaning to experiences which the child has already had, and may also help to define behaviour patterns for the future.

It is through listening to stories, and talking about the characters and events in them, that children first extend their understanding and ideas about their relationships with their peers, with adults, and with their made environment.

The involvement of children with the story can be very powerful; they will spontaneously transfer themes and characters into their own play sessions, and are frequently found acting out parts of stories that they have read, or have heard. This close identification with 'other' characters in 'other' situations can provide a useful and meaningful starting point for activities in Design and Technology.

Attainment Target 1 can provide something of a 'cold start' for most young children in terms of identifying needs and opportunities, and Attainment Target 4 can often be a more useful and fruitful starting point in the process of developing ideas and evaluating their outcomes. By focusing on a situation as it is, and evaluating items and events as they present themselves in the story, children are then able to consider other possibilities and alternatives.

It is only when we exercise a degree of empathy that we can begin to recognize what the needs of others might be. Also, when children have a clear vision of an environment, they can manipulate it mentally, and recognize opportunities for change and for improvement.

Children will often display a greater feeling of being in control of their actions, and the outcomes of those actions, when they use the story environment and its characters as a starting point for identifying needs and opportunities. It is important, however, that they feel able to transfer these skills to other 'real' contexts. So part of the evaluation process involves the children being encouraged to think how they might use these same ideas with people and in places that they are familiar with. For example, with the marble container for Roger several children were able to suggest alternative uses for such a container, or were able to suggest items of their own or belonging to members of their families, which were constantly being misplaced, and thought of devices or containers which they could make to prevent this.

It's Your Turn, Roger!
Susanna Gretz
In this story Roger climbs the staircase in the apartment block in which he lives, visiting other families. At the end of the story Roger runs back down the staircase enticed by the aroma of his supper coming up the stairs.

We looked carefully at the illustration of the staircase, and thought about ways in which we could construct a similar one. The brief was straightforward – 'Can you make a staircase for Roger?'

Developing and using artefacts, systems and environments
After looking at the illustration of Roger's staircase in the story, the children looked around the classroom for different materials with which to build a staircase. They found and used various kinds of construction equipment, wooden building bricks, cuisenaire rods, dominoes and books. This was an important prerequisite to constructing their final staircase as it helped them to see how the stairs were formed by a regular pattern, and that the top of the staircase needed to be supported underneath or it would fall over.

Working with materials

After experimenting with construction equipment and other found components, the children were given a choice of paper, card and sticky tape to work with. As they had previously used three-dimensional components to make their staircases, they were now having to use sheet material and form it into three-dimensional structures. Their experiences with the construction equipment were particularly supportive here, as the children had already identified the need to form a regular zig-zag with the card in order to create the steps. It is sometimes demanding for a young child to transfer two-dimensional images into three dimensions, and the construction equipment can provide a supportive link between the two stages. The child has a means of making a concrete statement about spatial concepts available to her.

Children who used paper to build with quickly found its structural properties inadequate, and rejected it in favour of a more resistant card. They were asked questions such as:

- Why does the staircase bend in the middle? Can you find a way to make it straight?
- Can you build a wall next to the staircase?
- Can you make a door for Roger to go through?
- Can you make Roger and put him on the stairs? Which way is he going?

In this way the children were continually trying different ways to manipulate the materials they were using. Some children also wanted to use resistant materials to support their staircases, and used short pieces of section timber to do this.

Developing and communicating ideas

While the children were able to extend the initial model that they made through the questions that were asked, they were also encouraged to think of their own ideas for improving the staircase. One of the ideas that the children generated from the story was through the smells which had come up the stairs to Roger. Several children constructed these smells by using strands of wool. They defined a different smell for each colour of wool, and attached the end of these aromas to Roger's nose.

Design and Technology	Programme of Study *Developing and Communicating Ideas*

'Use imagination, and own experiences, to generate and explore ideas.'
'Represent and develop ideas by drawings, models, talking, writing, working with materials.'

Satisfying Needs and Addressing Opportunities

'Evaluate finished work against the original intention.'

Satisfying needs and addressing opportunities

As the children had not worked out their ideas through drawings in this activity, but through modelling and continual refinement, they evaluated their work against the ideas that they had discussed and tried out prior to using card, paper and sticky tape to build a model. They were asked to assess the staircase in terms of its appearance, its scale in relation to the model of Roger that they had made, its structural durability, and the

Design and Technology	Programme of Study *Satisfying Needs and Addressing Opportunities*
'Evaluate finished work against original intention.'	

range of materials which they had used. One final suggestion was that if a lift was made for Roger then he would not need to have a staircase at all, and it might be quicker for him to get up and down the building.

Roger Loses his Marbles
Susanna Gretz

Having established a relationship with Roger, it seemed sensible to consider Roger's needs through another of his stories. In this story Roger's aunt comes to stay, and helps Roger to find his long-lost marbles. After reading the story the children looked at ways of preventing

Roger from losing his marbles again. The children discussed ways in which they looked after their own marbles at home, and the variety of containers they used.

The children then thought about the materials which were available to them in school to make a container, and what form that container might take.

The criteria for the container were identified by the children prior to planning the artefact through drawing. The marbles had to be held in by the container; it had to be strong enough to hold them – the children weighed the class collection of marbles in their hands and agreed they were quite heavy – it should be attractive; it had to be constructed out of available materials.

Developing and communicating ideas

The children were asked to plan their container by drawing it out on paper. After they had finished their preliminary plan each child was asked questions about their proposals. The questions asked, and their answers, were written on their drawings so that the children had a record of their thoughts, as well as their visual ideas. It was also useful to refer back to some of these statements later in the process to remind the children of their earlier ideas, and give them an opportunity to justify any changes and refinements that they made.

Design and Technology	Programme of Study *Developing and Communicating Ideas*
'Represent and develop ideas by drawings, models, talking, writing, working with materials.'	

When the children started to use the drawings to help them make their artefact, they used the drawing as a scale-representation, and tended to measure their work against their drawings. They found the use of their drawing as a pattern useful and supportive.

Working with materials

The children used a variety of resistant and non-resistant materials for their work, for example, felt and wool, card, plastic and timber. They used sticky tape, hot glue, and sewing to join the materials together. Where hot glue was specified, this was carried out by the teacher while the children watched. Even though some drawings were used as patterns, the children found that accuracy in cutting and joining edges together was important; gaps would allow marbles to escape.

Design and Technology	Programme of Study *Working with Materials*
'Join materials and components in a simple way.' 'Use materials and equipment safely.' 'Explore and use a variety of materials to design and make things.'	

Ashley wrote 'Roger's Bag' on his felt bag with felt tip pens, while others decorated their containers with pens, crayons, and buttons.

Satisfying needs and addressing opportunities
Initially the children's thoughts and ideas were expressed verbally, and recorded by the teacher on their drawings. After completing their container they tested it with a collection of marbles and talked to the rest of the class about their work. This post-activity talking is important for the children in terms of developing their skills in addressing an audience, expressing their thoughts and ideas, and describing processes and materials that they have used, enabling them to clarify their own understanding of the activity. It also enables the teacher to assess levels of understanding, competency and enjoyment, which are all-important factors in terms of planning future activities to provide progression. If the finished artefact bears little resemblance to the planned appearance this may not be important. What is important is that the child is able to discuss and justify any changes and refinements which they may have made during the course of the manufacturing process.

The Giant Jam Sandwich
John Vernon Lord and J Burroway
This story was used to support topic work about food. The children had decided that the role-play area in the classroom would be a sandwich bar, and part of their planning for this was a discussion about how to make a sandwich. If the children were going to be involved in 'making' and 'selling' sandwiches, then they would have to consider the correct sequencing procedure for this.

Developing and using artefacts, systems and environments
As a starting point for this activity, the children listened to the story, and discussed the order of events leading up to the sandwich being finished. While there were parts of the sequence in the story that were not relevant to their own needs (for example, making and baking the bread), the children were able to identify the main features of the sequence which they needed. They were also able to identify a feature which did not form part of the story, that is, the need to have clean hands before handling food.

It is only through analysis of a sequence in retrospect

Design and Technology	Programmes of Study *Developing and Using Artefacts, Systems and Environments*
'Give a sequence of instructions to produce a desired result.' 'Identify what should be done and ways in which work should be organized.'	

that children are able to develop the skill, and understand the importance of forward planning in terms of logical ordering and the sequencing of actions. A story can provide valuable support through this process, enabling the children to refer continually to the process, and consider the reasons for that order.

Working with materials
While the materials that the children would be using to make sandwiches in the role-play area would be synthetic, it was supportive to their understanding of the process to use the real thing as an initial activity.

The children drew up a list of necessary equipment and materials for the activity, and considered ways in which they would record their observations for future reference.

Design and Technology	Programmes of Study *Working with Materials*
'Recognize that materials are processed in order to change or control their properties.'	

The story introduced the children to the process of making and baking bread, and they decided that they would like to carry this activity through at a later stage. They made their jam sandwiches following their proposed order of activity, and then made suggestions for alternative materials which could be used as sandwich components in the role-play area.

Developing and communicating ideas
The order of the sandwich-making sequence was printed out with the computer, and illustrated by different children. It was useful to them to have this as a visual reference in the sandwich bar, and reinforced the vocabulary of sequencing: First . . ., then . . ., next . . ., last of all . . .

From this the children were able to identify the manufacturing sequence for other kinds of sandwiches which they had decided to 'sell' as well.

Design and Technology	Programmes of Study *Developing and Communicating Ideas*
'Represent and develop ideas by drawings, models, talking, writing, working with materials.' 'Find out, sort, store and present information for use in designing and making.'	

Satisfying needs and addressing opportunities
With this activity, the children were addressing their own needs and using the story context to help them satisfy those needs. The story was was both a starting point for identifying their needs, and a source of

'Know that goods are bought, sold and advertised.'
'Evaluate finished work against the original intention.'

technical information on how to satisfy those needs. The children first had to assess what the needs of the users were, and then adapt those criteria to their own. They were also able to transfer these skills to making other resources for their sandwich bar: the consideration of necessary materials, and the ordering of the task in a logical and efficient order.

Evaluation of activities in terms of national curriculum attainment targets

	THE GIANT JAM SANDWICH	ROGER LOSES HIS MARBLES	IT'S YOUR TURN, ROGER!
AT 4	Reading the story: evaluating the process of making sandwiches	Reading the story: evaluate Roger's needs for his marbles	Reading the story evaluate Roger's staircase
AT 1	Can we plan our own needs for making sandwiches?	Can we make something to help Roger keep his marbles safe?	Can we make a staircase for Roger?
AT 2	Identification of criteria and plan for recording of sequence	Generate proposals through discussion and drawing	Use construction equipment and drawings to plan staircase
AT 3	Printing and illustrating the sequencing chart	Manufacture the proposed containers	Construct own staircase using card/timber and sticky tape
AT 4	Evaluation using the chart to guide sandwich making process	Test with marbles and evaluate against original intentions	Evaluate finished system in terms of strength and appearance

CLASSROOM ORGANIZATION

Non-statutory guidance for Design and Technology states that 'Pupils need access to a variety of materials and tools, to make choices for themselves. Pupils should see what is available; scanning resources helps to stimulate ideas. Equipment and materials should be organized, accessible and labelled' (Section B 2.12).

In a perfect world children would have access to the widest possible range of tools and materials, in a classroom with abundant space and storage facilities. This is a rare situation and teachers are committed to organizing the materials and tools that children do have access to in whatever space is available.

In the early years children need to have access to, and an understanding of, a comprehensive rather than an extensive range of tools and materials with which to work. As their skills and understanding develop, their access to a range of resources should increase in tandem. It is therefore important that curriculum planning ensures that this development is supported. Children will need to have a wide experience of non-resistant materials such as clay, paper, and fabric, using modelling tools and scissors efficiently and appropriately before using resistant materials.

As children become experienced with a widening range of resources, it will be helpful to them to know where and how those resources are stored. Not only will they have a visual reminder of choice, but they will be independent in making it. They will also need this information so that they can clear away properly at the end of their activity.

If there is not room in the classroom to store and display the full range of available materials it might be more practical to use a samples box or board showing the range of sheet materials, fabrics, papers, and so on that the children can use. If resources are stored out of sight then the children can be introduced to them through planned activities. For example, manufactured storage systems which incorporate small plastic drawers are a very useful way to store small components for joining materials, such as paper clips, elastic bands, split pins, and treasury tags. The children will need to be challenged to investigate the contents of these with a planned activity such as the train building or washing line activity. Children need constant support and encouragement in becoming independent workers, and the more accessible the resources are for them, the more likely this will be. Their choices can only be appropriate however, if they have a clear grasp of the way those resources will behave and work for them.

If children are developing these skills and this level of autonomy in the early years it seems sensible to ensure that it will be continued throughout their time in school. A corporate approach to storage and resources will support this. If a drawer storage system is used for the same range of components throughout the school then the child will be able to locate these items in any teaching area without asking for support. The development of this level of autonomy is not only important in promoting independence in the child, it has implications for the way the teacher spends her time working with the children during these activities.

In many schools the children contribute towards the supply of materials by bringing recycled packaging and containers into the classroom from home. It is important not to refer to this material as 'junk'; this has negative implications for any work which they do with it, and is environmentally undesirable. The issue of recycling can be discussed with the children so that they regard these items as valuable. It can be their responsibility to sort and store them appropriately.

Before the children are able to develop the same level of autonomy in using a range of tools, they will need clear guidance in how to use them safely and correctly. It can be useful to demonstrate the correct way to hold a tool such as a saw, and the correct way to stand while sawing, to the whole class, but then to work with a small group of three or four children to ensure close supervision. Parent helpers and ancillary help can be a valuable source of support here but these helpers may themselves require the same level of support before working with the children. The development of good practice at this stage will stay with the children throughout their time in school if consistently supported.

Children will need to be reminded from time to time about the correct way to hold a tool, just as some children need to be reminded to hold their pencil properly. They may also need to be reminded about the availability of resources. This can be supported by sending the children to 'find' things.

A bank of cards can be made; one set for materials, one for tools, one for components. The child is given a card and asked to find the item or items written on it. The card only serves as a reminder for the teacher, and it is not necessary for the child to be able to read it.

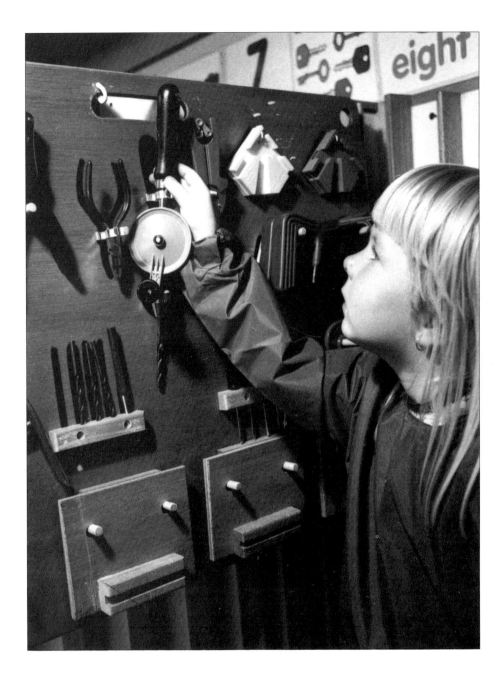

Examples of materials cards
- a sample of something to make a purse with
- a sample of something to make a flag with
- a sample of something to wrap a present in
- something to make rough timber smooth

Examples of tools cards
- something to make a hole in paper
- something to cut a piece of timber
- something to make a pattern in clay
- something to help draw a straight line

Examples of components cards
- a way of joining two pieces of paper
- something to use as a wheel
- a way of joining two pieces of fabric

These investigations can be given to a group of children to enable a range of possible solutions to be seen. Each child in the group has to find something different to everyone else if possible.

If the children are going to be encouraged to use the classroom environment in this way, it might also be important for them to be involved in any decisions about reorganization and relocation. If it is their classroom, and their resources, then it is important that they are encouraged to think about the arrangement and location of resources within it.

ASSESSMENT, EVALUATION AND RECORDING

The attainment targets in Design and Technology outline the criteria for assessment of skills, knowledge and understanding. While children are developing these skills, knowledge and understanding, it is possible that the activities they are involved in are not directly related to those attainment targets. The attainment targets in Design and Technology are unique in their relationship with each other, and cannot be viewed as separate areas of development: they represent a continuous process which may not necessarily begin with Attainment Target 1.

Planning by the teacher is important as it is necessary to ensure the provision of experiences which will develop the relevant skills, knowledge and understanding in a meaningful way. The Programmes of Study provide the framework for this planning, enabling activities to be broad and balanced, as well as providing continuity and progression. The skills, knowledge, and understanding developed through these activities will enable children to deal confidently and competently with the process embodied in the attainment targets.

Assessment can take several forms, and serves a variety of purposes. It can be carried out by the teacher and by the child.

Teacher assessment

Teacher assessment will enable close monitoring of curriculum planning in terms of the range and quality of experiences offered to the children. It will also enable the teacher to evaluate learning and achievement. The criteria which have guided planning will therefore also provide a useful basis for this assessment.

- Have the activities built on previous experiences?
- Have they introduced new concepts in a meaningful context?
- Have the activities provided experiences in which the children can develop new skills as well as consolidate those that have been previously experienced?
- Have the activities extended their understanding of materials in terms of behavioural properties and appropriate applications?
- Have the activities enabled the children to work in a variety of groupings, for example, individually, in small groups, as a whole class?
- Have the activities encouraged the children to develop a range of ideas within each context?
- Have the activities enabled them to develop their skills in identifying needs and addressing opportunities?
- Is there a balance of activities which will enable the children to experience the process inherent in the four attainment targets, as well as activities which support the development of specific technological skills and concepts, and those which do both?

- Do the activities offer the children the opportunity to work with a range of materials and media, for example, food, resistant materials, textiles, and graphic media?

In assessing the learning and achievement of the individual child the criteria will be more specific. Some evidence of this may be found in the product of an activity, but this will not inform the teacher about the child's ability to work cooperatively or independently; their ability to overcome difficulties encountered; their response to materials and resources; or their ability to appraise and refine.

None of the criteria outlined above are intended to be seen as a 'check list' for the teacher to fill in during, or at the end of, an activity. They are intended to guide judgement and the need to draw conclusions about the developmental progress of an individual child.

Self assessment by the child

While the first two statements above are clearly distinct in that the first one deals with the child assessing the product of an activity, and the second with the assessment of the process, the two are inextricably linked in the way that they support the child's understanding of the whole design and technology experience.

With the very young child particularly, but with older children too, it is only through describing and discussing their ideas, their intentions, their actions, and their feelings about their work that they are able to clarify their thoughts, and form coherent conclusions about the activities in which they have been engaged.

Design and Technology	Programme of Study Satisfying Needs and Addressing Opportunities
	'Evaluate finished work against the original intention.' 'Talk about what they have done during their designing and making.' 'Talk about what they have learnt and what they might do differently next time.' 'Reflect, individually and in groups, on how they went about their work, and whether changes might be needed.'

Children should be given the opportunity to talk about their work frequently. This may be work concerned with other curriculum areas and not only Design and Technology.

Just as talking through a mathematical activity can help to clarify and consolidate a mathematical concept, talking about the way that they have used a particular material in a technological activity can help their understanding of the behavioural properties of that material. Because this can become part of the normal pattern of class activity, the children become confident

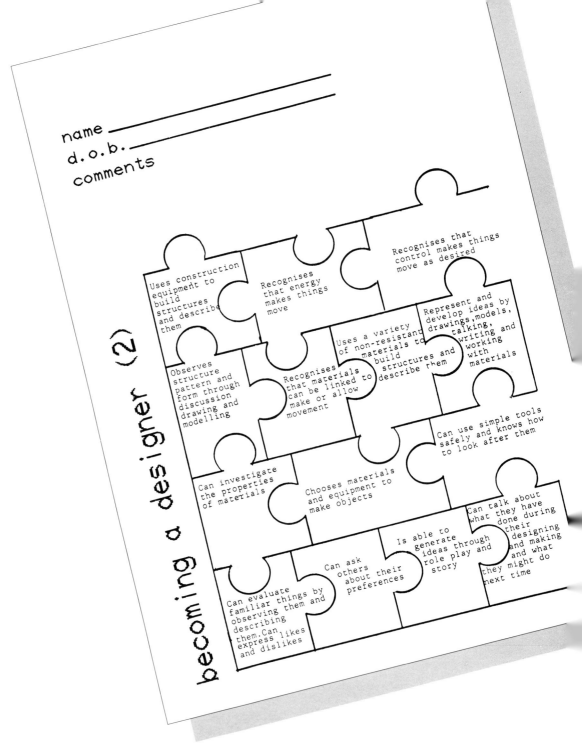

name _____

d.o.b. _____

comments

becoming a designer (2)

Uses construction equipment to build structures and describe them

Recognises that energy makes things move

Recognises that control makes things move as desired

Observes structure pattern and form through discussion and drawing and modelling

Recognises that materials can be linked to make or allow movement

Uses a variety of non-resistant materials to build structures and describe them

Represent and develop ideas by drawings, models, talking, writing and working with materials

Can investigate the properties of materials

Chooses materials and equipment to make objects

Can use simple tools safely and knows how to look after them

Can evaluate familiar things by observing them and describing them. Can express likes and dislikes

Can ask others about their preferences

Is able to generate ideas through role play and story

Can talk about what they have done during their designing and making and what they might do next time

speakers to an audience, and develop their skills in describing and justifying their activities.

This part of the activity can also provide valuable insights for the teacher, enabling assessment of the child's understanding about what they have done, their level of enjoyment, and also highlight any areas in which they have experienced difficulty. It can also be an aid to other children in the class as it provides them with information, examples of techniques, and ideas.

Many of the statements of attainment in each attainment target rely on children's ability to express, describe, discuss, comment and explain. Evidence of attainment is dependent on the development of these skills: the children having the ability to demonstrate their understanding, their ideas, their preferences and their actions through language. It is through continuous experience that they will be able to do this.

Becoming a designer

It may be supportive to curriculum planning to record areas of experience that children have met within the framework of the Programme of Study. When children come into the reception class time must be spent assessing their present level of experience and understanding before planning can be effectively and accurately directed towards their needs.

There may be some indication of levels of achievement at the point of transition if the child has come from a nursery, and this will provide valuable information to support future provision. If there is an on-site nursery, then it is more useful to liaise with staff there, and develop a recorded means of passing on information at the point of transition.

Becoming a designer (1) is a record form developed for this purpose by one particular school. The areas of

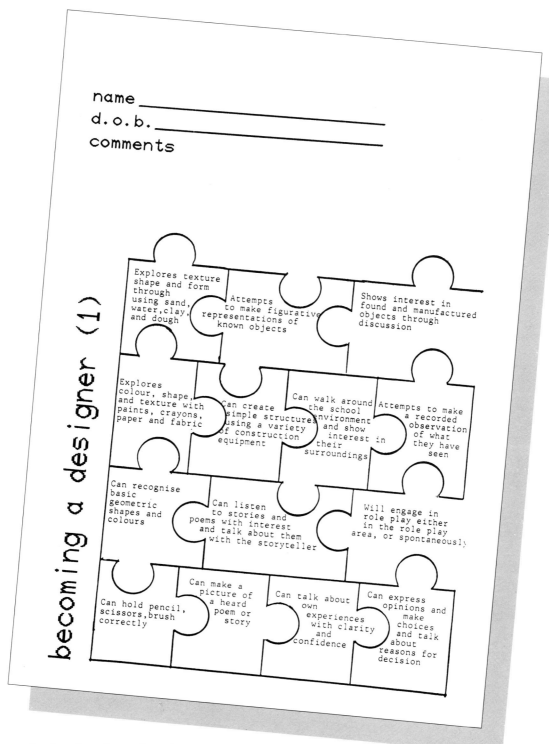

name_____

d.o.b._____

comments_____

becoming a designer (1)

Explores texture shape and form through using sand, water, clay, and dough

Attempts to make figurative representations of known objects

Shows interest in found and manufactured objects through discussion

Explores colour, shape, and texture with paints, crayons, paper and fabric

Can create simple structures using a variety of construction equipment

Can walk around the school environment and show interest in their surroundings

Attempts to make a recorded observation of what they have seen

Can recognise basic geometric shapes and colours

Can listen to stories and poems with interest and talk about them with the storyteller

Will engage in role play either in the role play area, or spontaneously

Can hold pencil, scissors, brush correctly

Can make a picture of a heard poem or story

Can talk about own experiences with clarity and confidence

Can express opinions and make choices and talk about reasons for decision

activity are interrelated, and are drawn from the elements outlined in the Key Stage 1 Programme of Study. These elements are then broken down into activities which are appropriate to the nursery child. It may also be useful to nursery colleagues to be able to identify those activities which support the development of skills and understanding in design and technology.

Becoming a designer (2) provides continuity to this record, enabling the activities and experiences to relate directly to those in the Key Stage 1 Programme of Study, ensuring that each child has a broad and balanced curriculum. The experiences on both sheets are generally sequential, moving from top left towards bottom right-hand corners. By shading in these areas as the child responds positively and competently to this experience, the teacher is able to build up an overall record of the child's development.

BIBLIOGRAPHY

Early Years Curriculum Group (1989) *Early Childhood Education: The Early Years Curriculum and the National Curriculum*. Trentham Books.

Gretz, S (1985) *It's Your Turn, Roger!* Bodley Head.

Gretz, S (1988) *Roger Loses His Marbles*. Bodley Head.

Kelly, A V et al (1987) *Design and Technological Activity: A Framework for Assessment*. HMSO.

Lancaster, J (ed) (1986) *Art Craft and Design in the Primary School*. NSEAD.

Lord, J V and Burroway, J (1972) *The Giant Jam Sandwich*. Jonathan Cape.

Manning, K and Sharp, A (1977) *Structuring Play in the Early Years at School*. (Schools Council Project) Ward Lock.

Morgan, M (ed) (1988) *Art in the First Years of Schooling*. Blackwell.

Pluckrose, H A (1989) *Store It; Cut It; Joint It; Move It; Wear It*. Franklin Watts.

Thistlewood, D (ed) (1990) *Issues in Design Education*. Longman.